Miss Bea's Dressing up

Louisa Harding

ROWAN

'We're dressing up today'.
Miss Bea ties the ribbons of her ballet shoes.

Hannah swirls and twirls,
swishing her grass skirt and paper flowers.

'Can you tell me where it Hurts?'
Miss Bea listens to teddy's heartbeat.

Innes finds a quiet corner,
he is reading from his book of spells.

Miss Bea guards the treasure chest,
'keep away you naughty pirates'.

Tinkerbell sweater instructions page 36

'Yo ho ho, I've found the gold',
Sol looks at all the treasures.

Pirate Jacket instructions page 38

In a feather crown and gloves,
Hannah wonders which jewels to try on.

Innes builds a camp fire,
'Howdy there' he says.

Sheriff Jacket instructions page 42

Miss Bea sits down a while
and warms up by the fire.

'Round up the horses' Sol says
'It's time to go now, yee ha'.

Cowboy Waistcoat instructions page 46

The Knitting Patterns
Infomation Page

Introduction

The knitwear in 'Miss Bea's Dressing Up' has been designed using the intarsia technique, this enables the knitter to add pattern to the knitting by introducing new colours. With beginner knitters in mind we have included a visual guide to intarsia knitting on page 27.

The knitting patterns

Each pattern has a chart and simple written instructions that have been colour coded making the different sizes easier to identify. E.g. if you are knitting age 2–3 years follow the instructions in red where you are given a choice. The patterns are laid out as follows:

Age/Size Diagrams

The ages given and the corresponding diagrams are a guide only. The measurements for each knitted piece are shown in a size diagram at the start of every pattern. As all children vary make sure you choose the right garment size, do this by measuring an item of your child's clothing you like the fit of. Choose the instruction size accordingly. If still unsure, knit a larger size, as children always grow.

Yarn

This indicates the amount of yarn needed to complete the design. All the garments use more than one colour so you will have an amount for each shade used.

Needles

Listed are the suggested knitting needles used to make the garment. The smaller needles are usually used for edgings or ribs, the larger needles for the main body fabric.

Buttons/Zips

This indicates the number of buttons or length of zip needed to fasten the finished garment.

Tension

Tension is the single most important factor when you begin knitting. The fabric tension is written for example as 20 sts x 28 rows to 10cm measured over stocking stitch using 4 mm (US 6) needles. Each pattern is worked out mathematically, if the correct tension is not achieved the garment pieces will not measure the size stated in the diagram.

Before embarking on knitting your garment we recommend you check your tension as follows: Using the needle size given cast on 5 –10 more stitches than stated in the tension, and work 5 –10 more rows. When you have knitted your tension square lay it on a flat surface, place a rule or tape measure horizontally, count the number of stitches equal to the distance of 10cm. Place the measure vertically and count the number of rows, these should equal the tension given in the pattern.

If you have too many stitches to 10cm, try again using a thicker needle, if you have too few stitches to 10cm use a finer needle.

Note: Check your tension regularly as you knit, once you become relaxed and confident with your knitting, your tension can change.

Back

This is the start of your pattern. Following the colour code for your chosen size, you will be instructed how many stitches to cast on and to work from chart and written instructions as follows:

Knitting from charts

Each square on a chart represents one stitch; each line of squares indicates a row of knitting. When working from the chart, read odd numbered rows (right side of fabric) from right to left and even numbered rows (wrong side of fabric) from left to right.

Each separate colour used is given a letter and on some charts a corresponding symbol. The different stitches used are also represented by a symbol, e.g. knit and purl, a key to the symbols is with each chart.

Front (Fronts) and Sleeves

The pattern continues with instructions to make these garment pieces.

Pressing

Once you have finished knitting and before you begin to complete the garment it is important that all pieces are pressed, see page 48 for more details.

Neckband (Front bands)

This instruction tells you how to work any finishing off needed to complete your garment, such as knitting a neckband on a sweater or edgings on a cardigan. Once you have completed all the knitting you can begin to make up your garment, see page 48 for making up instructions.

Abbreviations

In the pattern you will find some of the most common words used have been abbreviated, these are listed below:

K	knit
P	purl
st(s)	stitches
inc	increase(e)(ing) knit into the front and back of next stitch, making 2 stitches.
dec	decreas(e)(ing)
st st	stocking stitch (right side row knit, wrong side row purl)
garter st	garter stitch (knit every row)
beg	begin(ning)
foll	follow(ing)
rem	remain(ing)
rev	reverse(ing)
rep	repeat
alt	alternate
cont	continue
patt	pattern
tog	together
cm	centimetres
in(s)	inch(es)
RS	right side
WS	wrong side
K2tog	knit two sts together to make one stitch
tbl	through back of loop
yo	yarn over, bring yarn over needle before working next st to create an extra loop.

Knitting Techniques
A simple learn to knit guide

Introduction

Using illustrations and simple written instructions we have put together a beginners guide to knitting. With a basic knowledge of the simplest stitches you can create your own unique handknitted garments.

When you begin to knit you feel very clumsy, all fingers and thumbs. This stage passes as confidence and experience grows. Many people are put off hand knitting thinking that they are not using the correct techniques of holding needles, yarn or working of stitches, all knitters develop their own style, so please persevere.

Casting On

This is the term used for making a row of stitches; the foundation row for each piece of knitting. Make a slip knot. Slip this onto a needle. This is the basis of the two casting on techniques as shown below.

Thumb Cast On

This method uses only one needle and gives a neat, but elastic edge. Make a slip knot 1 metre from the cut end of the yarn, you use this length to cast on the stitches. For a knitted piece, the length between cut end and slip knot can be difficult to judge, allow approx 3 times the width measurement.

1. Make a slip knot approx 1 metre from the end of the yarn, with ball of yarn to your right.

2. Hold needle in RH. With the cut end of yarn held in LH, wrap yarn around your thumb from left to right anti-clockwise to front.

3. Insert RH needle into yarn around thumb, take yarn attached to ball around the back of RH needle to front.

4. Draw through needle to make a loop.

5. Pull on both ends of yarn gently. Creating a stitch on right hand needle.

6. Repeat from 2. until the required number of stitches has been cast on.

Cable Cast On

This method uses two needles; it gives a firm neat finish. It is important that you achieve an even cast on, this may require practice.

1. With slip knot on LH needle, insert RH needle. Take yarn behind RH needle; bring yarn forward between needles.

2. Draw the RH needle back through the slip knot, making a loop on RH needle with yarn.

3. Slip this loop onto left hand needle; taking care not to pull the loop too tight.

4. Insert the RH needle between the two loops on LH needle. Take yarn behind RH needle; bring forward, between needles.

5. Draw through the RH needle making a loop as before. Slip this stitch onto LH needle.

6. Repeat from 4. until the required number of stitches has been cast on.

How to Knit –
The knit stitch is the simplest to learn. By knitting every row you create garter stitch and the simplest of all knitted fabrics.

1. Hold the needle with the cast-on stitches in LH. Insert RH needle into first stitch.

2. Take yarn around the back of RH needle, bring yarn forward between needles.

3. Draw the RH needle through the stitch. Drop loop on LH needle

4. Making a loop on RH needle with yarn. One stitch made.

5. Repeat to the end of the row.

How to Purl –
The purl stitch is a little more complicated to master. Using a combination of knit and purl stitches together forms the bases of most knitted fabrics. The most common fabric knitted is stocking stitch, this is created when you knit 1 row, then purl 1 row.

1. Hold the needle with stitches on in LH and with yarn at the front of work, insert RH needle into front of stitch.

2. Take yarn around the back of RH needle, bring yarn to front.

3. Draw the needle through from front to back, making a loop on RH needle.

4. Slip the stitch onto right hand needle. Drop loop on LH needle.

5. Repeat to the end of the row.

Joining in a new yarn –
A new ball of yarn can be joined in on either a right side or a wrong side row, but to give a neat finish it is important you do this at the start of a row. Simply drop the old yarn, start knitting with the new ball, then after a few stitches tie the two ends together in a temporary knot. These ends are then sewn into the knitting at the making up stage, see page 48.

Casting Off –
This is the method of securing stitches at the top of your knitted fabric. It is important that the cast off edge should be elastic like the rest of the fabric; if you find that your cast off is too tight, try using a larger needle. You can cast off knitwise (as illustrated), purlwise, or in a combination of stitches, such as rib.

1. Hold the needle with the stitches on in LH, knit the first stitch.

2. Knit the next stitch from LH needle, two stitches on RH needle.

3. Using the point of LH needle; insert into first stitch on RH needle.

4. Take the first stitch over the second stitch.

5. One stitch on right hand needle.

6. Rep from 2. until one stitch on RH needle. Cut yarn, draw cut end through last stitch to secure.

Intarsia Knitting – Intarsia is the name given to knitting with more than one colour in a row. You will need to use a separate length of yarn for each area of colour. There can be any number of colours used per row but the patterns in Miss Bea's Dressing Up have been designed to start you off gently.

We have used the Intarsia technique for simple motifs, such as spots, hearts and flowers and in colour blocks, horizontal and diagonal stripes. All the designs in the book have a chart, each separate colour is given a letter and a corresponding symbol. Where there is a symbol change this indicates a change of colour.

It is essential when you are changing colour that you twist the two yarns around each other, otherwise you will create two separate pieces of knitting. By twisting the yarns you prevent a hole from forming, but remember to **always** cross the yarns over on the wrong side of your work.

Where two or more colours are used in a row it can be difficult to avoid tangling the yarns, use short lengths of yarn or bobbins as these can be pulled through easily.

An example of vertical line colour change – This technique ensures that the yarns are crossed on every row, and gives a neat, unbroken vertical line on the right side.

On a right side row – work to the colour change, make sure both yarns are at the back of the work, drop the first colour, pick up the second colour and bring it across the first colour to cross the yarns over before working the next stitch.

On a wrong side row – make sure both yarns are at the front (WS) of the work, drop the first colour, pick up the second colour and bring it around the first colour before working the next stitch.

An example of a spot motif colour change – Using the same technique as above of twisting the yarns around each other on the wrong side of the work. On a chart this colour change is indicated by a change of symbol.

On a right side row – work to the colour change, make sure both yarns are at the back of the work, drop the first colour, pick up the second colour and bring it across the first colour to cross the yarns over before working the next stitch. Intoduce a new strand of yarn for each colour change.

On a wrong side row – make sure both yarns are at the front (WS) of the work, drop the first colour, pick up the second colour and bring it around the first colour before working the next stitch. Work the first stitch in each colour firmly to avoid a gap forming between the colours.

Finishing off – With the Intarsia technique there will be yarn ends to sew in at the end of your knitting, do this by threading the yarn onto a sewing-up needle. Thread each yarn end into the same colour along the loops formed by the yarn twists on the wrong side of knitting. Fasten off neatly.

Ballerina Cardigan

Age 1-2 years   2-3 years   3-4 years

Size

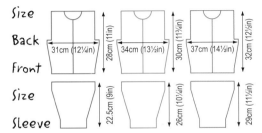

Back 31cm (12¼in)   34cm (13½in)   37cm (14½in)
28cm (11in)   30cm (11¾in)   32cm (12½in)

Front

Size

Sleeve 22.5cm (9in)   26cm (10¼in)   29cm (11½in)

Yarn

Rowan Handknit Cotton x 50g balls

A. Olive	5	5	5
B. Celery	1	1	1
C. Pink	1	1	1

Needles

1 pair 3 ¼ mm (US 3) needles for edging
1 pair 4mm (US 6) needles for main body

Buttons 5

Tension

20 sts and 28 rows to 10cm measured over stocking stitch using 4mm (US 6) needles

Note The argyll pattern is worked on cardigan fronts only.

Back

Using 3 ¼ mm (US 3) needles and yarn A, cast on 54,60,66 sts and work from chart and written instructions as folls:
Chart row 1: Knit.

Chart row 2: Knit.
Cont in garter st until chart row 6 completed.
Change to 4mm (US 6) needles and beg with a K row work 2 rows in st st from chart.
Chart row 9: Inc into first st, knit to last st, inc into last st. (56,62,68 sts)
Cont from chart shaping sides by inc as indicated to 62,68,74 sts.
Cont without shaping until chart row 44,46,50 completed.
Shape armhole
Cast off 6 sts at the beg next 2 rows.
(50,56,62 sts)
Cont until chart row 80,86,92 completed.
Shape shoulders and back neck
Cast off 4,4,5 sts at the beg next 2 rows.
Chart row 83,89,95: Cast off 4,4,5 sts, patt until 6,8,8 sts on RH needle, turn and leave rem sts on a holder.
Chart row 84,90,96: Cast off 3 sts, patt to end.
Cast off rem 3,5,5 sts.
Rejoin yarn and cast off centre 22,24,26 sts, patt to end. (10,12,13 sts)
Chart row 84,90,96: Cast off 4,4,5 sts, patt to end. (6,8,8 sts)
Chart row 85,91,97: Cast off 3 sts, patt to end.
Cast off rem 3,5,5 sts.

Left Front

Using 3 ¼ mm (US 3) needles and yarn A, cast on 27,30,33 sts and work from chart and written instructions as folls:
Chart row 1: Knit.
Chart row 2: Knit.
Cont in garter st until chart row 6 completed.
Change to 4mm (US 6) needles and beg with a K row, work 2 rows in patterned st st from chart, joining in and breaking off colours as required and using the intarsia technique for argyll pattern as illustrated on page 27.
Chart row 9: Inc into first st, patt to end.
(28,31,34 sts)
Cont from chart, keeping patt correct and shaping side edge by inc as indicated to 31,34,37 sts.
Work without further shaping until chart row 44,46,50 completed.
Shape armhole
Cast off 6 sts at the beg next row. (25,28,31 sts)
Work without further shaping until chart row 75,81,87 completed.
Shape front neck
Chart row 76,82,88: Cast off 8,9,10 sts, patt to end. (17,19,21 sts) Work 1 row.
Chart row 78,84,90: Cast off 4 sts, patt to end.
Dec 1 st at neck edge on next 2 rows. (11,13,15 sts)

Shape shoulder
Cast off 4,4,5 sts at the beg next row and foll alt row.
Work 1 row. Cast off rem 3,5,5 sts.

Right Front

Using 3 ¼ mm (US 3) needles and yarn A, cast on 27,30,33 sts and work from chart and written instructions as folls:
Chart row 1: Knit.
Chart row 2: Knit.
Cont in garter st until chart row 6 completed.
Change to 4mm (US 6) needles and complete to match left side foll chart for right front and reversing shaping.

Sleeves (both alike)

Using 3 ¼ mm (US 3) needles and yarn A, cast on 34,36,38 sts and work from chart and written instructions as folls:
Chart row 1: Knit.
Chart row 2: Knit.
Cont in garter st until chart row 6 completed.
Change to 4 mm (US 6) needles and beg with a K row cont in st st as folls:
Chart row 7: Inc into first st, knit to last st, inc into last st. (36,38,40 sts)
Chart row 8: Purl to end.
Cont from chart, shaping sides by inc as indicated to 52,56,60 sts.
Work without further shaping until chart row 66,74,84 completed.   Cast off.

Press all pieces as shown on page 48.

Buttonhole band

With RS of right front facing and using 3 ¼ mm (US 3) needles and yarn A, pick up and knit 54,58,62 sts from cast on edge to start of neck shaping.
Row 1 (WS row): Knit
Buttonhole row (RS row): K2, (K2tog, yo, K10,11,12 4 times, K2tog, yo, K2. Knit 1 row.
Leave these sts on a holder.

Buttonband

With RS of right left facing and using 3 ¼ mm (US 3) needles and yarn A, pick up and knit 54,58,62 sts from start of neck shaping to cast on edge.
Knit 3 rows. Leave these sts on a holder.

Neckband

Join both shoulder seams using backstitch.
With RS facing and using 3 ¼ mm (US 3) needles and yarn A pick up and knit 3 sts across buttonhole band,

,17,18 sts up right front neck shaping,
,30,32 sts across back neck, and
,17,18 sts down left front neck, and 3
s from buttonband. (66,70,74 sts)

ow 1 (WS row): knit
uttonhole row (RS row): K1, yo,
2tog, knit to end.
nit 1 row.
hange to yarn C and knit 1 row.
ast off knitwise using yarn C.

uttonhole band
ith RS of right front facing and using
¼ mm (US 3) needles and yarn C knit
,60,64 sts on holder, pick up 4 sts
om neck band. (58,64,68 sts)
ast off knitwise using yarn C.

utton band
ith RS of right front facing and using
¼ mm (US 3) needles and yarn C pick
 4 sts from neck band, knit across
,60,64 sts on holder. (58,64,68 sts)
ast off knitwise using yarn C.
omplete cardigan as shown on page 48.
w on buttons to correspond with
uttonholes.
sing yarn C embroider a daisy
to each of the diamonds as in the
otograph.

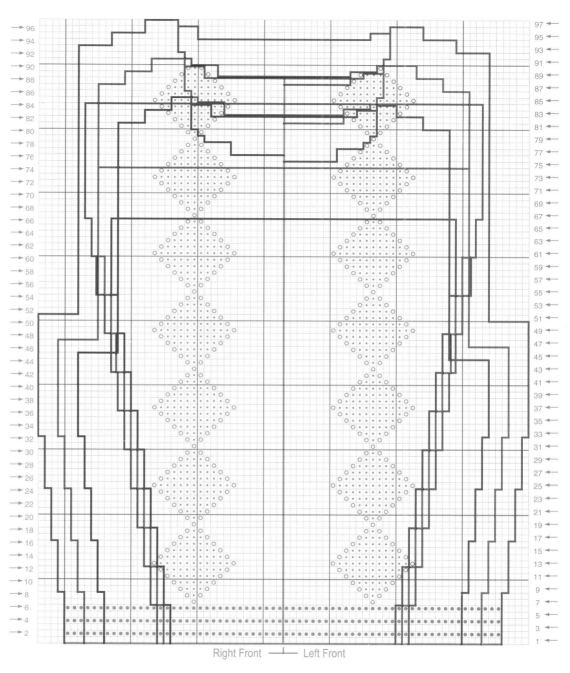

Right Front ⊢ Left Front

| | Yarn A K on RS, P on WS | | Yarn A P on RS, K on WS | | Yarn B K on RS, P on WS | | Yarn C K on RS, P on WS | Argyll panels worked on fronts only |

Hula Hula Sweater

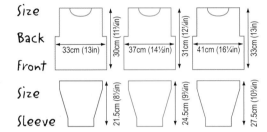

	Age	1-2 years	2-3 years	3-4 years
Size	Back	33cm (13in) / 30cm (11¾in)	37cm (14½in) / 31cm (12¼in)	41cm (16¼in) / 33cm (13in)
Front				
Size	Sleeve	21.5cm (8½in)	24.5cm (9¾in)	27.5cm (10¾in)

Yarn

Rowan Wool Cotton x 50g balls

A. Violet	3	4	4
B. Purple	1	1	1
C. Lilac	1	1	1
D. Citron	1	1	1

Needles

1 pair 3 ¼ mm (US 3) needles for edging
1 pair 4mm (US 6) needles for main body

Tension

22 sts and 30 rows to 10cm measured over patterned
stocking stitch using 4 mm (US 6) needles

Back

Using 3 ¼ mm (US 3) needles and yarn A, cast
on 73,81,89 sts and work from chart and written
instructions as folls:
Chart row 1: Knit.
Chart row 2: Knit.
Cont in garter st from chart until row 10 completed
Change to 4mm (US 6) needles and beg with a K row
cont in st st, joining in and breaking off colours as

required and using the intarsia technique for border
pattern as illustrated on page 27.
Work from chart until row 52,54,58 completed.
Shape armhole
Cast off 6 sts at the beg next 2 rows. (61,69,77 sts)
Work until chart row 92,96,102 completed.
Shape shoulders and back neck
Cast off 5,6,7 sts at the beg next 2 rows.
Chart row 95,99,105: Cast off 5,6,7 sts, knit until 7,8,9
sts on RH needle, turn and leave rem sts on a holder.
Chart row 96,100,106: Cast off 3 sts, purl to end.
Cast off rem 4,5,6 sts.
Slip centre 27,29,31 sts onto a holder, rejoin yarn to
rem sts and knit to end. (12,14,16 sts)
Chart row 96,100,106: Cast off 5,6,7 sts, purl to end.
(7,8,9 sts)
Chart row 97,101,107: Cast off 3 sts, knit to end.
Cast off rem 4,5,6 sts.

Front

Work as for back until chart row 88,92,98 completed.
Shape front neck
Chart row 89,93,99: Knit 20,23,26 sts, turn and leave
rem sts on a holder.
Chart row 90,94,100: Cast off 4 sts, purl to end.
(16,19,22 sts)
Dec 1 st at neck edge on next 2 rows. (14,17,20 sts)
Shape Shoulder
Cast off 5,6,7 sts at beg next row and foll alt row.
Purl 1 row.
Cast off rem 4,5,6 sts.
Slip centre 21,23,25 sts onto a holder, rejoin yarn to
rem sts and knit to end. (20,23,26 sts)
Purl 1 row
Chart row 91,95,101: Cast off 4 sts, knit to end.
Dec 1 st at neck edge on next 2 rows. (14,17,20 sts)
Shape shoulder
Cast off 5,6,7 sts at beg next row and foll alt row.
Knit 1 row.
Cast off rem 4,5,6 sts.

Sleeves (both alike)

Using 3 ¼ mm (US 3) needles and yarn A, cast
on 37,39,41 sts and work from chart and written
instructions as folls:
Chart row 1: Knit.
Chart row 2: Knit.
Cont in garter st from chart until row 10 completed
Change to 4mm (US 6) needles and yarn B.
Chart row 11: Inc into first st, knit to last st, inc into
last st. (39,41,43 sts)
Chart row 12: Using yarn D, purl.

Cont in patterned st st, joining in and breaking off
colours as required and using the intarsia technique for
border pattern **at the same time** shape sides by inc as
indicated to 57,61,65 sts.
Work without further shaping until chart row 66,76,84
completed.
Cast off.

Press all pieces as shown in making up instructions,
page 48.

Neckband

Join right shoulder seam using backstitch.
Using 3 ¼ mm (US 3) needles and yarn A pick up and
knit 10 sts down left front neck, knit across 21,23,25
sts on holder, pick up and knit 10 sts to shoulder and
sts down right back neck, knit across 27,29,31 sts on
holder, pick up and knit 3 sts to shoulder. (74,78,82 sts)
Rib row 1 (WS row): Knit.
Rib row 2 (RS row): Knit.
Work these 2 rows 3 times more.
Cast off knitwise.
Complete sweater as shown in making up instructions,
page 48, leaving 10 rows at bottom edge open.

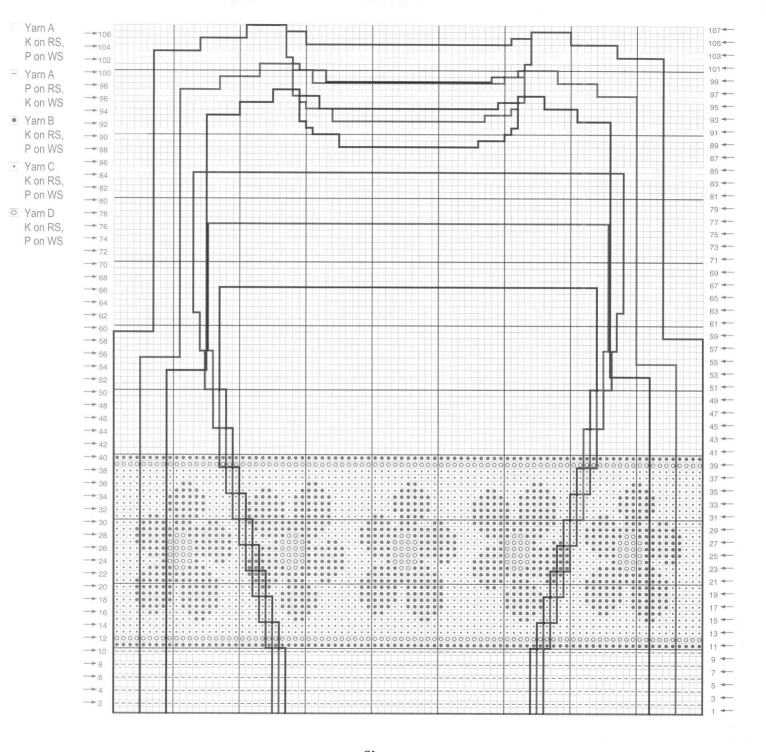

Yarn A
K on RS,
P on WS

Yarn A
P on RS,
K on WS

Yarn B
K on RS,
P on WS

Yarn C
K on RS,
P on WS

Yarn D
K on RS,
P on WS

31

Doctor Cardigan

Age 1-2 years   2-3 years   3-4 years

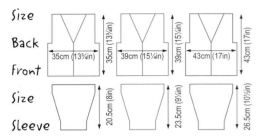

Size Back Front — 35cm (13¾in), 35cm (13¾in), 39cm (15¼in), 39cm (15¼in), 43cm (17in), 43cm (17in)

Size Sleeve — 20.5cm (8in), 23.5cm (9¼in), 26.5cm (10½in)

Yarn
Rowan All Seasons Cotton x 50g balls

A. Cookie	5	6	6
B. Purple	1	1	1

Needles
1 pair 4 mm (US 6) needles for edging
1 pair 5 mm (US 8) needles for main body

Buttons 5

Tension
17 sts and 24 rows to 10cm measured over stocking stitch using 5mm (US 8) needles

Note Heart motifs are worked on fronts only.

Back
Using 4 mm (US 6) needles and yarn A cast on 60,66,72 sts and work from chart and written instructions as folls:
Chart row 1: Knit.
Chart row 2: Knit.
Cont in garter st until chart row 6 completed.
Change to 5mm (US 8) needles and beg with a K row cont in stocking stitch from chart until row 52,60,68

completed.
Shape armhole
Cast off 5 sts at the beg next 2 rows. (50,56,62 sts)
Work until chart row 86,96,106 completed.
Shape shoulder and back neck
Chart row 87,97,107: Cast off 5,5,6 sts at the beg next 2 rows.
Chart row 89,99,109: Cast off 5,5,6 sts, knit until 7,9,9 sts on RH needle, turn, leave rem sts on a holder.
Chart row 90,100,110: Cast off 3 sts, purl to end. Cast off rem 4,6,6 sts.
Cast off centre 16,18,20 sts, rejoin yarn to rem sts and knit to end. (12,14,15 sts)
Chart row 90,100,110: Cast off 5,5,6 sts beg next row, purl to end.
Chart row 91,101,111: Cast off 3 sts, knit to end. Cast off rem 4,6,6 sts.

Front Pocket Linings (work 2)
Using 5 mm (US 8) needles cast on 18 sts and beg with a K row work 24 rows in st st. Leave sts on a holder.

Left Front
Using 4 mm (US 6) needles and yarn A cast on 30,33,36 sts and work from chart and written instructions as folls:
Chart row 1: Knit.
Chart row 2: Knit.
Cont in garter st until chart row 6 completed.
Change to 5mm (US 8) needles and beg with a K row cont in st st from chart until row 10 completed.
Joining in and breaking off colours as required and using the intarsia technique work heart motif as illustrated on page 27 as folls:
Row 11: Using yarn A, K13,16,19, using yarn B, K1, using yarn A, K16.
Row 12: Using yarn A, P15, using yarn B, P3, using yarn A, P12,15,18.
Keeping patt correct cont until chart row 30 completed.
Chart row 31 (place pocket): Knit 5,8,11 sts, slip next 18 sts onto a holder, knit across 18 sts from first pocket lining, knit to end. (30,33,36 sts)
Cont until chart row 52,60,68 completed.
Shape armhole and front neck
Cast off 5 sts at the beg next row, knit to last 2 sts, K2tog. (24,27,30 sts)
Cont to dec at neck edge as indicated to 14,16,18 sts.
Work without further shaping until chart row 86,96,106 completed.
Shape shoulder
Cast off 5,5,6 sts at the beg next row and foll alt row.
Work 1 row.
Cast off rem 4,6,6 sts.

Right Front
Using 4 mm (US 6) needles and yarn A cast on 30,33,36 sts and work from chart and written instructions as folls:
Chart row 1: Knit.
Chart row 2: Knit.
Cont in garter st until chart row 6 completed.
Change to 5mm (US 8) needles and beg with a K row cont in st st from chart until row 10 completed.
Joining in and breaking off colours as required and using the intarsia technique work heart motif as folls:
Row 11: Using yarn A, K16, using yarn B, K1, using yarn A, K13,16,19.
Row 12: Using yarn A, P12,15,18, using yarn B, P3, using yarn A, P15.
Keeping patt correct cont until chart row 30 completed.
Complete to match left front, foll chart for right front, reversing shaping and placing of pocket.

Sleeves (both alike)
Using 4 mm (US 6) needles cast on 30,32,34 sts and work from chart and written instructions as folls:
Chart row 1: Knit.
Chart row 2: Knit.
Cont in garter st until chart row 6 completed.
Change to 5 mm (US 8) needles and beg with a K row cont in st st from chart as folls:
Chart row 7: Inc into first st, knit to last st, inc into last st. (32,34,36 sts)
Chart row 8: Purl.
Cont from chart, shaping sides by inc as indicated to 48,52,54 sts.
Work without further shaping until chart row 52,58,66 completed.
Cast off.

Press all pieces as shown in making up instructions on page 48.

Front bands
Join both shoulder seams using backstitch.
With RS of right front facing and using 4 mm (US 6) needles pick up and knit 36,40,44 sts from cast on edge to start of neck shaping, 30,32,35 sts up right front neck slope to shoulder, 21,24,25 sts across back neck, 30,32,35 sts down left front neck slope, and 36,40,44 sts to end.
(153,168,183 sts)
Work 2 rows in garter st ending with a RS row.
Work picot cast off as follows: Cast off 3 sts, *slip st on RH needle back onto LH needle, cast on 2 sts using the cable method, then cast off 5 sts, rep from * to end.

Pocket tops (both alike)

With RS facing slip 18 sts left on pocket holder onto 4mm (US 6) needle. Rejoin yarn, work 3 rows in garter st ending with a RS row.

Work picot cast off as follows: Cast off 3 sts, *slip st on RH needle back onto LH needle, cast on 2 sts using the cable method, then cast off 5 sts, rep from * to end.

Complete jacket as shown on page 48.

Sew 5 buttons to left front, the first to come 2 cm up from lower edge, last to come 1 cm down from start of front slope shaping and rem 3 buttons spaced evenly between.

To fasten buttons, push them through small hole made in picot cast off on right front.

☐ Yarn A
K on RS,
P on WS

⊡ Yarn A
P on RS,
K on WS

● Yarn B
K on RS,
P on WS

Heart motif
worked on
fronts only

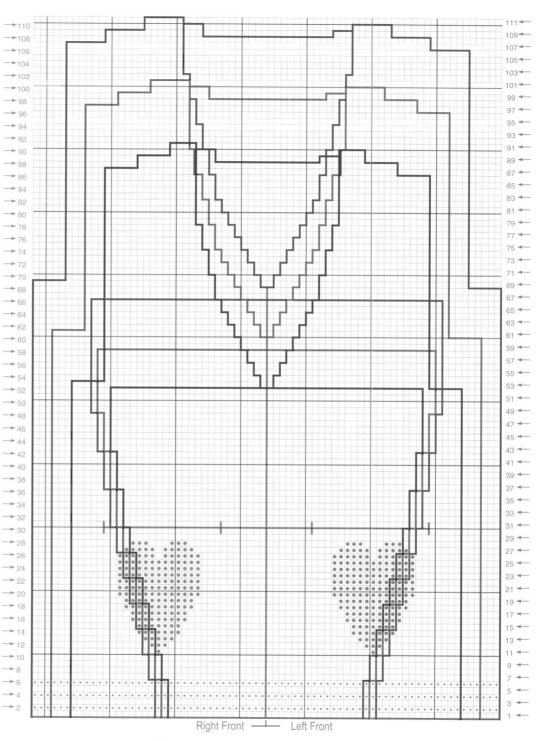

Right Front ——— Left Front

33

Wizard Sweater

Age 1-2 years   2-3 years   3-4 years

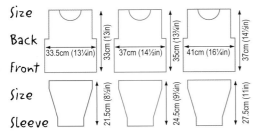

Size
Back

33.5cm (13¼in)   33cm (13in)   37cm (14½in)   35cm (13¾in)   41cm (16¼in)   37cm (14½in)

Front

Size
Sleeve

21.5cm (8½in)   24.5cm (9¾in)   27.5cm (11in)

Yarn
Rowan All Seasons Cotton x 50g balls

A. Misty	5	5	5
B. Cream	1	1	1
C. Charcoal	1	1	1

Needles
1 pair 4mm (US 6) needles for rib
1 pair 5mm (US 8) needles for main body

Tension
17 sts and 24 rows to 10cm measured over stocking stitch using 5mm (US 8) needles

Back
Using 4mm (US 6) needles and yarn C cast on 57,63,69 sts and work from chart and written instructions as folls:
Chart row 1: K3,0,3, (P3, K3) to last 0,3,0 sts, P0,3,0.
Chart row 2: P3,0,3, (K3, P3) to last 0,3,0 sts, K0,3,0.
Change to yarn A and cont in rib until chart row 10 completed.
Change to 5mm (US 8) needles and beg with a K row cont in st st from chart, joining in and breaking off

colours as required and using the intarsia technique as illustrated on page 27, work until chart row 50,52,54 completed.
Shape armhole
Cast off 5 sts at the beg next 2 rows. (47,53,59 sts)
Work until chart row 80,84,88 completed.
Shape shoulders and back neck
Chart row 81,85,89: Knit 13,15,17 sts, turn and leave rem sts on a holder.
Chart row 82,86,90: Cast off 3 sts, purl to end.
Slip rem 10,12,14 sts onto a holder.
Slip centre 21,23,25 sts onto a holder, rejoin yarn to rem sts and knit to end. (13,15,17 sts)
Work 1 row
Chart row 83,87,91: Cast off 3 sts, knit to end.
Leave rem sts 10,12,14 onto a holder.

Front
Work as for back to chart row 74,78,82 completed.
Shape front neck
Chart row 75,79,83: Knit 16,18,20 sts, turn and leave rem sts on a holder.
Chart row 76,80,84: Cast off 4 sts, purl to end.
Dec 1 st at neck edge on next 2 rows.
(10,12,14 sts)
Work without further shaping until chart row 82,86,90 completed.
Slip rem 10,12,14 sts onto a holder.
Slip centre 15,17,19 sts onto a holder, rejoin yarn to rem sts and knit to end. (16,18,20 sts)
Work 1 row.
Chart row 77,81,85: Cast off 4 sts, knit to end.
Dec 1 st at neck edge on next 2 rows.
Leave rem sts 10,12,14 sts on a holder.

Sleeves (both alike)
Using 4mm (US 6) needles and yarn C cast on 29,31,33 sts and work from chart and written instructions as folls:
Chart row 1: K1,2,3, (P3, K3) to last 4,5,6 sts, P3, K1,2,3.
Chart row 2: P1,2,3, (K3, P3) to last 4,5,6 sts, K3, P1,2,3.
Change to yarn A and cont in rib until chart row 10 completed.
Change to 5mm (US 8) needles and beg with a K row cont in st st, joining in and breaking off colours as required and using the intarsia method, work from chart as folls:
Chart row 11: Inc into first st, K to last st, inc into last st. (31,33,35 sts)
Chart row 12: Purl.

Cont from chart shaping sides by inc as indicated to 45,47,51 sts.
Work without further shaping until chart row 54,60,68 completed.
Cast off.

Press all pieces as shown in making up instructions, page 48.

Neckband
Using yarn A join right shoulder seam by knitting sts together on the RS of garment as shown in knitting techniques guide, page 48.
Using 4mm (US 6) needles pick up and knit 10,10,11 sts down left front neck, knit across 15,17,19 sts on holder, pick up and knit 10,10,11 sts to shoulder and 3 sts down right back neck, knit across 21,23,25 sts on holder and pick up and knit 3 sts to shoulder. (62,66,72 sts)
Rib row 1 (WS): K1,0,0, (K3, P3) to last 1,0,0 st, P1,0,0.
Rib row 2: K1,0,0, (K3, P3) to last 1,0,0 st, P1,0,0.
Work these 2 rows twice more.
Change to yarn C and work 2 rows in rib.
Cast off in rib.
Join left shoulder seam by knitting sts together on the RS of garment as above using yarn A.
Join neckband seam using backstitch.
Complete sweater as shown in making up instructions page 48.

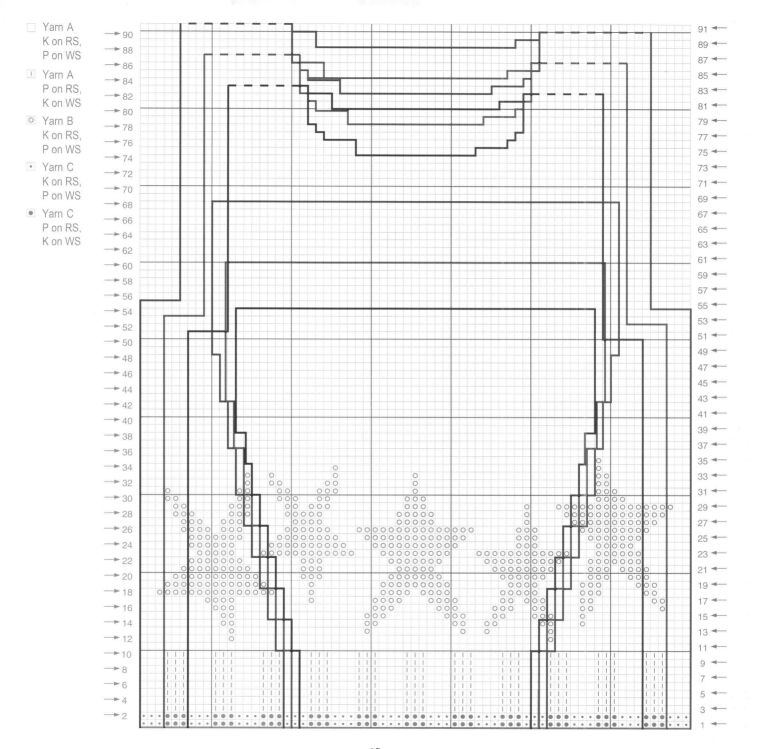

Tinkerbell Sweater

Age 1-2 years 2-3 years 3-4 years

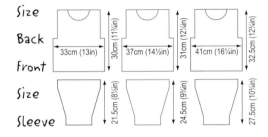

Size			
Back	33cm (13in)	37cm (14½in)	41cm (16¼in)
	30cm (11¾in)	31cm (12¼in)	32.5cm (12¾in)

Front

Size			
Sleeve	21.5cm (8½in)	24.5cm (9¾in)	27.5cm (10¾in)

Yarn
Rowan All Seasons Cotton x 50g balls

A. Purple	5	5	5
B. Lilac	1	1	1
C. Ice	1	1	1

Needles
1 pair 4mm (US 6) needles for edging
1 pair 5mm (US 8) needles for main body

Tension
17 sts and 24 rows to 10cm measured over stocking stitch using 5mm (US 8) needles

Note Flower motif is worked on front of sweater only

Back
Using 4mm (US 6) needles and yarn C cast on 57,63,69 sts and work from chart and written instructions as folls:
Chart row 1: Knit.
Chart row 2: Knit.
Change to yarn A, cont as folls:
Chart row 3: Knit.

Chart row 4: P1,0,1, (K1, P1) to last 0,1,0 sts, K0,1,0.
Chart row 5: P1,0,1, (K1, P1) to last 0,1,0 sts, K0,1,0.
Cont in moss st until chart row 10 completed.
Change to 5mm (US 8) needles and beg with a K row cont in stocking stitch until chart row 44,44,46 completed.
Shape armhole
Cast off 5 sts at the beg next 2 rows. (47,53,59 sts)
Cont until chart row 76,78,82 completed.
Shape shoulders and back neck
Cast off 3,4,5 sts at beg next 2 rows.
Chart row 79,81,85: Cast off 3,4,5 sts, knit until 7 sts on RH needle, turn and leave rem sts on a holder.
Chart row 80,82,86: Cast off 3 sts, purl to end.
Cast off rem 4 sts.
Slip centre 21,23,25 sts onto a holder, rejoin yarn to rem sts and knit to end. (10,11,12 sts)
Chart row 80,82,86: Cast off 3,4,5 sts, purl to end.
Chart row 81,83,87: Cast off 3 sts, knit to end.
Cast off rem 4 sts.

Front
Work as for back to chart row 20 completed.
Now joining in and breaking off new colours as required using the intarsia technique, as illustrated on page 27, work central flower motif from chart as folls:
Chart row 21: K30,33,36 sts using yarn A, join in yarn B and K4 sts, join in another length of yarn A and K23,26,29 sts.
Chart row 22: P22,25,28 sts using yarn A, P6 sts using yarn B and P29,32,35 sts using yarn A.
Cont to work from chart as indicated until chart row 72,74,78 completed.
Shape front neck
Chart row 73,75,79: Knit 16,18,20 sts, turn and leave rem sts on a holder.
Chart row 74,76,80: Cast off 4 sts, purl to end.
Dec 1 st at neck edge on next 2 rows.
(10,12,14 sts)
Shape shoulder
Cast off 3,4,5 sts at beg next row and foll alt row.
Work 1 row.
Cast off rem 4 sts.
Slip centre 15,17,19 sts onto a holder, rejoin yarn to rem sts and knit to end. (16,18,20 sts)
Chart row 74,76,80: Purl 1 row.
Chart row 75,77,81: Cast off 4 sts, knit to end.
Dec 1 st at neck edge on next 2 rows. (10,12,14 sts)
Shape shoulder
Cast off 3,4,5 sts at beg next row and foll alt row.
Work 1 row.
Cast off rem 4 sts.

Sleeves (both alike)
Using 4mm (US 6) needles and yarn C cast on 29,31,33 sts and work from chart and written instructions as folls:
Chart row 1: Knit.
Chart row 2: Knit.
Change to yarn A and work in moss st as folls:
Chart row 3: Knit.
Chart row 4: P1,0,1, (K1, P1) to last 0,1,0 sts, K0,1,0.
Chart row 5: P1,0,1, (K1, P1) to last 0,1,0 sts, K0,1,0.
Cont in moss st until chart row 10 completed.
Change to 5mm (US 8) needles and cont in st st as folls:
Chart row 11: Inc into first st, knit to last st, inc into last st. (31,33,35 sts)
Chart row 12: Purl.
Cont from chart, shaping sides by inc as indicated to 45,47,51 sts.
Work without further shaping until chart row 56,62,70 completed.
Cast off.

Press all pieces as shown in making up instructions, page 48.

Neckband
Join right shoulder using backstitch.
Using 4mm (US 6) needles and yarn A pick up and knit 10 sts down left front neck, knit across 15,17,19 sts on holder, pick up and knit 10 sts to shoulder and 3 sts down right back neck, knit across 21,23,25 sts on holder and pick up and knit 3 sts to shoulder. (62,66,70 sts)
Edging row 1 (WS): K1,P1 to end.
Edging row 2: P1,K1 to end.
Work these 2 rows once more, then row one again.
Change to yarn C and knit 3 rows ending with a RS row.
Cast off knitwise.
Join left shoulder and neck edging using back stitch.
Complete sweater as shown in making up instructions, page 48.

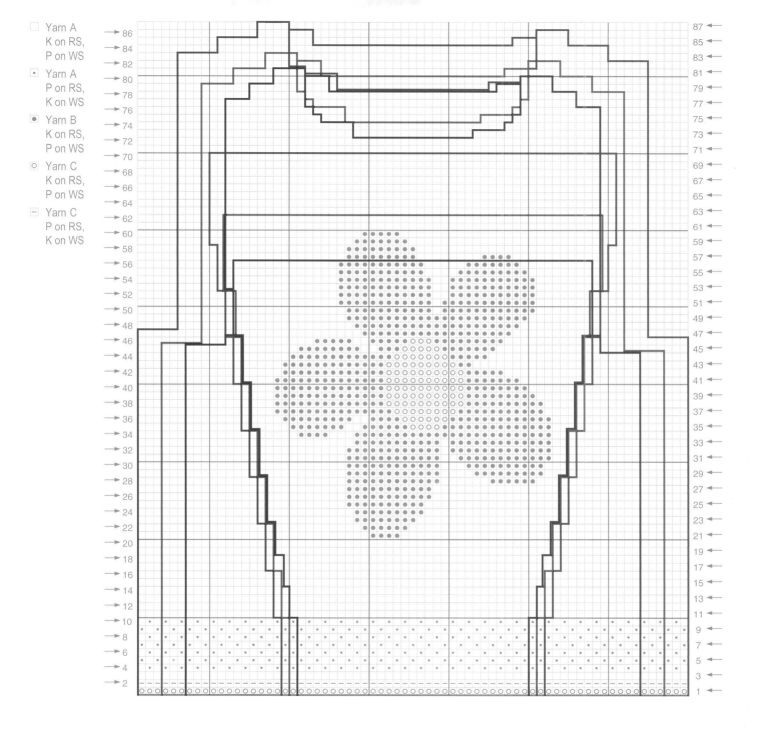

Pirate Jacket

Age 1-2 years 2-3 years 3-4 years

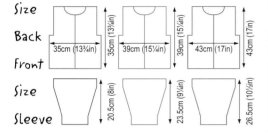

Size Back Front
35cm (13¾in) 35cm (13¾in) 39cm (15¼in) 39cm (15¼in) 43cm (17in) 43cm (17in)

Size Sleeve
20.5cm (8in) 23.5cm (9¼in) 26.5cm (10½in)

Yarn
Rowan All Seasons Cotton x 50g balls
A. Dusky   4   5   5
B. Cookie   2   2   2

Needles
1 pair 4 mm (US 6) needles for edging
1 pair 5 mm (US 8) needles for main body

Zip Open-ended zip to fit

Tension
17 sts and 24 rows to 10cm measured over stocking stitch using 5mm (US 8) needles

Back
Using 4 mm (US 6) needles and yarn A cast on 60,66,72 sts and work from chart and written instructions as folls:
Chart row 1: K0,2,0, P1,2,1, (K4, P2) 9,10,11 times, K4,2,4, P1,0,1.
Chart row 2: K1,0,1, P4,2,4, (K2, P4) 9,10,11 times, K1,2,1, P0,2,0.
Cont in rib until chart row 10 completed.

Change to 5mm (US 8) needles beg with a K row cont in patterned st st, joining in and breaking off colours as required and using the intarsia technique for spot motifs as illustrated on page 27.
Work from chart until row 52,60,68 completed.
Shape armhole
Cast off 5 sts at the beg next 2 rows.
(50,56,62 sts)
Work until chart row 84,94,104 completed.
Shape shoulders and back neck
Chart row 85,95,105: Patt 17,19,21 sts, turn and leave rem sts on a holder.
Chart row 86,96,106: Cast off 3 sts, patt to end.
Slip rem 14,16,18 sts onto a holder.
Rejoin yarn to rem sts, cast off centre 16,18,20 sts, knit to end. (17,19,21 sts)
Work 1 row
Chart row 87,97,107: Cast off 3 sts, patt to end.
Slip rem 14,16,18 sts onto a holder.

Left Front
Using 4 mm (US 6) needles and yarn A cast on 30,33,36 sts and work from chart and written instructions as folls:
Note: 3 sts at centre front are worked in garter st throughout and are **not** shown on chart.
Chart row 1: K0,2,0, P1,2,1, (K4, P2) 4,4,5 times, K5.
Chart row 2: K3, P2, (K2, P4) 4,4,5 times, K1,2,1, P0,2,0.
These 2 rows set the sts.
Cont in rib until chart row 10 completed.
Change to 5mm (US 8) needles and beg with a K row cont in patterned st st, joining in and breaking off colours as required and using the intarsia technique for spot motifs.
Cont to work until row 52,60,68 completed.
Shape armhole
Cast off 5 sts at the beg next row. (25,28,31 sts)
Work without further shaping until chart row 77,87,97 completed.
Shape front neck
Chart row 78,88,98: K3, P2,3,4 sts and leave these 5,6,7 sts on a holder, patt to end.
(20,22,24 sts)
Work 1 row.
Chart row 80,90,100: Cast off 4 sts beg next row, patt to end.
Dec 1 st at neck edge on next 2 rows.
(14,16,18 sts)
Work without further shaping until chart row 86,96,106 completed.
Slip rem sts onto a holder.

Right Front
Using 4 mm (US 6) needles and yarn A cast on 30,33,36 sts and work from chart and follow written instructions as follows:
Note: 3 sts at centre front are worked in garter st throughout and are **not** shown on chart.
Chart row 1: K5, (P2, K4) 4,4,5 times, P1,2,1, K0,2,0.
Chart row 2: P0,2,0, K1,2,1, (P4, K2) 4,4,5 times, P2, K3
These 2 rows set the sts.
Cont in rib until chart row 10 completed.
Change to 5mm (US 8) needles complete to match left front, foll chart for right front and reversing shaping.

Sleeves (both alike)
Using 4 mm (US 6) needles and yarn A cast on 30,32,34 sts and work from chart and written instructions as folls:
Chart row 1: K2,3,4, (P2, K4) 4 times, P2, K2,3,4.
Chart row 2: P2,3,4, (K2, P4) 4 times, K2, P2,3,4.
Cont in rib until chart row 10 completed.
Change to 5 mm (US 8) needles and beg with a K row cont in patterned st st, joining in and breaking off colours as required and using the intarsia technique for spot motifs.
Chart row 11: Inc into first st, knit to last st, inc into last st. (32,34,36 sts)
Chart row 12: Purl.
Cont from chart, shaping sides by inc as indicated to 48,52,54 sts.
Work without further shaping until chart row 52,58,66 completed.
Cast off.

Press all pieces as shown in making up instructions, page 48.

Neckband
Join both shoulder seams by knitting sts together on the RS of garment using yarn A, as shown in techniques guide, page 48.
With RS facing and using 4 mm (US 6) needles and yarn A, work in patt across 5,6,7 sts on holder at right front neck, pick up and knit 10 sts up right front neck shaping, 22,24,26 sts across back neck, 10 sts down left front neck, work in patt across 5,6,7 sts on holder.
(52,56,60 sts)
Rib row 1(WS): K3, (P2, K2) to last st, K1.
Rib row 2(RS): K3, (K2, P2) to last 5 sts, K5.
Rep these 2 rows 4 times more.
Cast off in rib.
Complete jacket as shown in making up instructions, page 48.

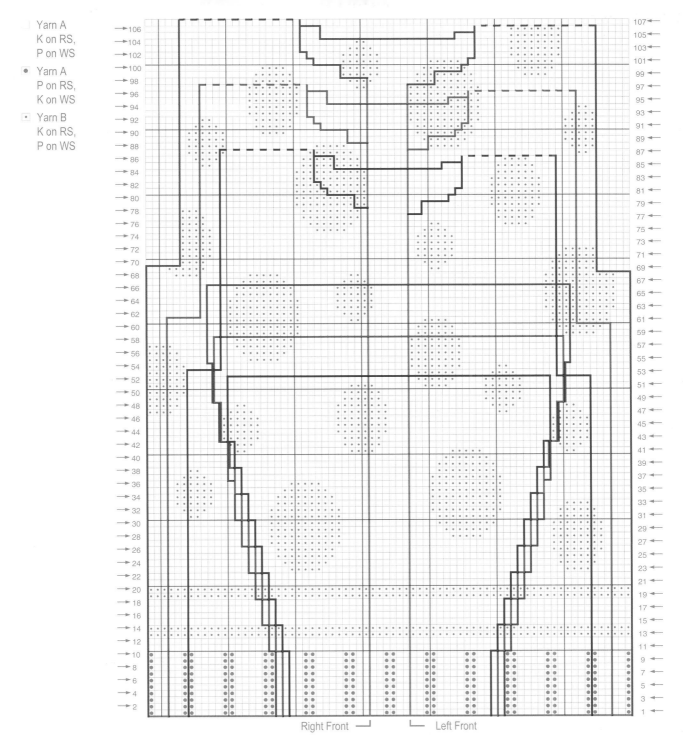

Yarn A
K on RS,
P on WS

Yarn A
P on RS,
K on WS

Yarn B
K on RS,
P on WS

Right Front

Left Front

39

Princess Cardigan

Age 1-2 years   2-3 years   3-4 years

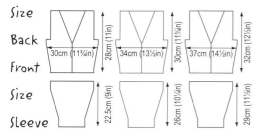

Size		
Back	30cm (11¾in), 28cm (11in)	34cm (13½in), 30cm (11¾in)	37cm (14½in), 32cm (12½in)
Front		
Size		
Sleeve	22.5cm (9in)	26cm (10¼in)	29cm (11½in)

Yarn

Rowan Wool Cotton x 50g balls

A. Ice Blue	2	2	2
B. Lilac	2	2	2
C. Violet	2	2	2

Needles

1 pair 3 ¼ mm (US 3) needles for edging
1 pair 4mm (US 6) needles for main body

Buttons 5

Tension

22 sts and 30 rows to 10cm measured over pattern st st using 4mm (US 6) needles

Back

Using 3 ¼ mm (US 3) needles and yarn A, cast on 56,64,72 sts and work from chart and written instructions as folls:
Chart row 1: Knit.
Chart row 2: Knit.
Cont in garter st until chart row 6 completed.
Change to 4mm (US 6) needles, beg with a K row cont

---

in st st, join in a separate length of yarn for each stripe using the intarsia technique, as illustrated on page 27 and shape sides as folls:
Chart row 7: Inc into first st, patt to last st, inc into last st. (58,66,74 sts)
Cont from chart shaping sides by inc as indicated to 66,74,82 sts.
Work without further shaping until chart row 46,50,54 completed.

Shape armhole
Cast off 6 sts at the beg next 2 rows.
(54,62,70 sts)
Cont in patt until chart row 86,92,98 completed.

Shape shoulders and back neck
Cast off 4,5,6 sts at the beg next 2 rows.
Chart row 89,95,101: Cast off 4,5,6 sts, patt until 7,8,9 sts on RH needle, turn and leave rem sts on a holder.
Chart row 90,96,102: Cast off 3 sts, patt to end.
Cast off rem 4,5,6 sts.
Rejoin yarn and cast off centre 24,26,28 sts, patt to end. (11,13,15 sts)
Chart row 90,96,102: Cast off 4,5,6 sts, patt to end.
(7,8,9 sts)
Chart row 91,97,103: Cast off 3 sts, patt to end.
Cast off rem 4,5,6 sts.

Left Front

Using 3 ¼ mm (US 3) needles and yarn A, cast on 28,32,36 sts and work from chart and written instructions as folls:
Chart row 1: Knit.
Chart row 2: Knit.
Cont in garter st until chart row 6 completed.
Change to 4mm (US 6) needles, beg with a K row cont in st st, join in a separate length of yarn for each stripe using the intarsia technique, and shape side as folls:
Chart row 7: Inc into first st, patt to end.
(29,33,37 sts)
Cont from chart, shaping side edge by inc as indicated to 33,37,41 sts.
Work without further shaping until chart row 46,50,54 completed.

Shape armhole and front neck
Cast off 6 sts at the beg next row, patt to last 2 sts, K2tog. (26,30,34 sts)
Cont to dec at neck edge as indicated to 12,15,18 sts.
Work without further shaping until chart row 86,92,98 completed.

Shape shoulder
Cast off 4,5,6 sts at the beg next row and foll alt row.
Work 1 row.
Cast off rem 4,5,6 sts.

Right Front

Using 3 ¼ mm (US 3) needles and yarn A, cast on 28,32,36 sts and work from chart and written instructions as folls:
Chart row 1: Knit.
Chart row 2: Knit.
Cont in garter st until chart row 6 completed
Change to 4mm (US 6) needles and complete to match left front following chart for right front and reversing shaping.

Sleeves (both alike)

Using 3 ¼ mm (US 3) needles and yarn A cast on 38,40,42 sts and work from chart and written instructions as folls:
Chart row 1: Knit.
Chart row 2: Knit.
Cont in garter st until chart row 6 completed.
Change to 4mm (US 6) needles, beg with a K row cont in st st, join in a separate length of yarn for each stripe using the intarsia technique, and shape sides as folls:
Chart row 7: Inc into first st, patt to last st, inc into last st. (40,42,44 sts)
Cont from chart, shaping sides by inc as indicated to 58,62,66 sts.
Work without shaping until chart row 70,80,90 completed.
Cast off.

Press all pieces as shown in making up instructions, page 48.

Frontband

Join both shoulder seams using backstitch.
With RS of right front facing and using 3 ¼ mm (US 3) needles and yarn A, pick up and knit 32,36,40 sts from cast on edge to start of neck shaping, 34,35,38 sts up right front neck slope to shoulder, 30,32,33 sts across back neck, pick up and knit 34,35,38 sts down left front neck slope, and 32,36,40 sts to end.
(162,174,189 sts)
Buttonhole row (WS): Knit 131,139,150 sts, (yo, K2tog, K5,6,7) 4 times, yo, K2tog, K1.
Knit 1 row.
Work picot cast off as folls: Cast off 3 sts, *slip st on RH needle back onto LH needle, cast on 2 sts using the cable method, then cast off 5 sts, rep from * to end.
Complete cardigan as shown in making up instructions, page 48.
Sew on buttons to correspond with buttonholes.

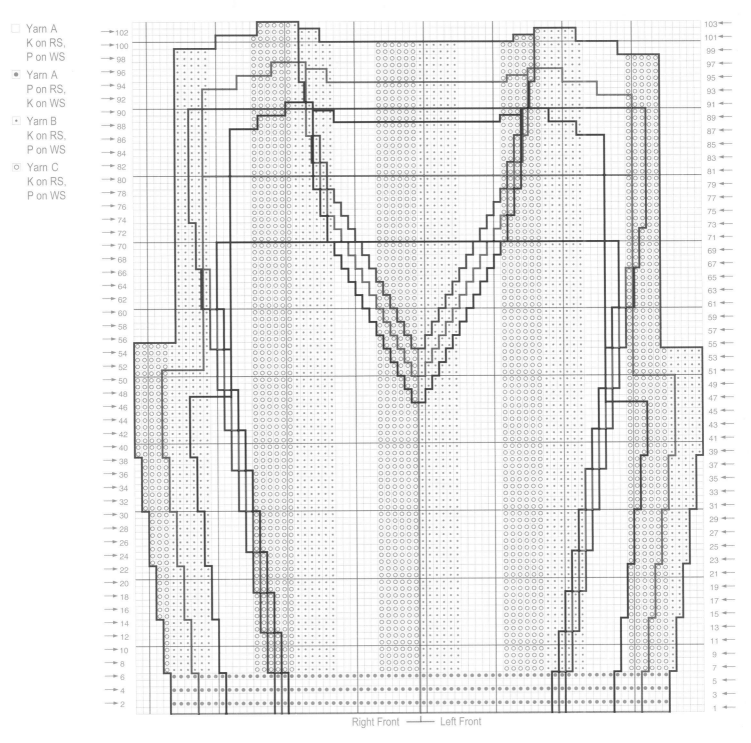

Yarn A
K on RS,
P on WS

Yarn A
P on RS,
K on WS

Yarn B
K on RS,
P on WS

Yarn C
K on RS,
P on WS

Right Front — Left Front

41

Sheriff Jacket

Age 1-2 years   2-3 years   3-4 years

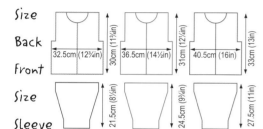

Size Back Front

32.5cm (12¾in)   30cm (11¾in)
36.5cm (14½in)
31cm (12¼in)   40.5cm (16in)   33cm (13in)

Size Sleeve

21.5cm (8½in)   24.5cm (9¾in)   27.5cm (11in)

Yarn

Rowan Handknit Cotton x 50g balls

A. Linen	4	4	5
B. Ice Water	2	2	2
C. Tope	1	1	1

Needles

1 pair 3 ¼ mm (US 3) needles for edging
1 pair 4mm (US 6) needles for main body

Buttons 5

Tension

20 sts and 28 rows to 10cm measured over patterned stocking stitch using 4 mm (US 6) needles

Back

Using 3 ¼ mm (US 3) needles and yarn B cast on 65,73,81 sts and work from chart A and written instructions as folls:
Chart row 1: K1, P1 to last st, K1.
Chart row 2: K1, P1 to last st, K1.
Cont in moss st until chart row 10 completed.
Change to 4 mm (US 6) needles and yarn A and beg

with a K row cont in st st until row 50,50,52 completed.
Shape armhole
Cast off 6 sts at the beg next 2 rows. (53,61,69 sts)
Now working from chart B, joining in and breaking off colours as required and using the intarsia technique as illustrated on page 27, cont in patt st st until chart row 34,36,40 completed.
Shape shoulders and back neck
Cast off 4,5,6 sts at the beg next 2 rows.
Chart row 37,39,43: Cast off 4,5,6 sts, patt until 8,9,10 sts on RH needle, turn and leave rem sts on a holder.
Chart row 38,40,44: Cast off 3 sts, patt to end.
Cast off rem 5,6,7 sts.
Rejoin yarn to rem sts, cast off centre 21,23,25 sts, patt to end. (12,14,16 sts)
Chart row 38,40,44: Cast off 4,5,6 sts, patt to end. (8,9,10 sts)
Chart row 39,41,45: Cast off 3 sts, patt to end.
Cast off rem 5,6,7 sts.

Left Front

Using 3 ¼ mm (US 3) needles and yarn B, cast on 30,34,38 sts and work from chart A and written instructions as folls:
Chart row 1: K1, P1 to end.
Chart row 2: P1, K1 to end.
Cont in moss st until chart row 10 completed.
Change to 4 mm (US 6) needles and yarn A and beg with a K row cont in st st until row 50,50,52 completed.
Shape armhole
Cast off 6 sts at the beg next row. (24,28,32 sts)
Now working from chart B, joining in and breaking off colours as required and using the intarsia technique cont in patt st st until chart row 29,31,35 completed.
Shape front neck
Chart row 30,32,36: Cast off 5,6,7 sts, patt to end. (19,22,25 sts)
Work 1 row.
Chart row 32,34,38: Cast off 4 sts, purl to end.
Dec 1 st at neck edge on next 2 rows. (13,16,19 sts)
Shape shoulders
Cast off 4,5,6 sts at the beg foll alt row.
Work 1 row
Cast off rem 5,6,7 sts.

Right Front

Using 3 ¼ mm (US 3) needles and yarn B cast on 30,34,38 sts and work from chart A and written instructions as folls:
Chart row 1: P1, K1 to end.
Chart row 2: P1, K1 to end.
Cont in moss st until chart row 10 completed.

Change to 4 mm (US 6) needles and yarn A and complete to match left front, foll chart for right front and reversing shaping.

Sleeves (both alike)

Using 3 ¼ mm (US 3) needles and yarn B, cast on 35,37,39 sts and work from chart A and written instructions as folls:
Chart row 1: K0,1,0, (P1, K1)to last 1,0,1 st, P1,0,1.
Chart row 2: K0,1,0, (P1, K1)to last 1,0,1 st, P1,0,1.
Cont in moss st until chart row 10 completed.
Change to 4 mm (US 6) needles and yarn A.
Chart row 11: Inc into first st, knit to last st, inc into last st. (37,39,41 sts)
Chart row 12: Purl.
Cont in st st from chart, shaping sides by inc as indicated to 53,57,61 sts.
Work without further shaping until chart row 62,70,80 completed. Cast off.

Press all pieces as shown in making up instructions, page 48.

Buttonband

With RS of right front facing and using 3 ¼ mm (US 3) needles and yarn B, pick up and knit 57,61,65 sts from cast on edge to start of neck shaping..
Row 1(WS): (K1,P1) to last st, K1.
Work 7 more rows in moss st.
Cast off knitwise.

Buttonhole band

With RS of left front facing and using 3 ¼ mm (US 3) needles and yarn B. pick up and knit 57,61,65 sts from start of neck shaping to cast on edge.
Row 1(WS): (K1,P1) to last st, K1.
Work 2 more rows in moss st.
Buttonhole row (RS): K1, P1, (yo, Patt 2tog, patt 11,12,13) 4 times, yo, Patt 2tog, K1.
Work 4 more rows in moss st.
Cast off knitwise.

Collar

Using 3 ¼ mm (US 3) needles and yarn B, cast on 67,71,75 sts.
Work 19,21,23 rows in moss st, ending with a RS row.
Cast off knitwise.
Join both shoulder seams using backstitch.
Sew cast on edge of collar to neck edge, matching row ends at front opening edges.
Complete as shown on page 48.
Sew on buttons to correspond with buttonholes.

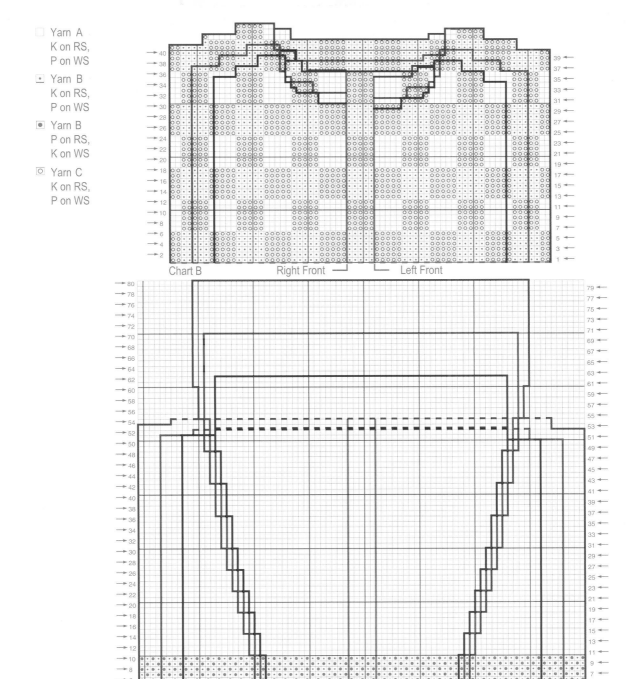

Yarn A
K on RS,
P on WS

Yarn B
K on RS,
P on WS

Yarn B
P on RS,
K on WS

Yarn C
K on RS,
P on WS

Chart B   Right Front   Left Front

Chart A   Right Front   Left Front

Little Indian Sweater

Age 1-2 years   2-3 years   3-4 years

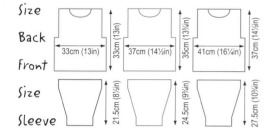

Size Back Front
33cm (13in)   37cm (14½in)   41cm (16¼in)
33cm (13in)   35cm (13¾in)   37cm (14½in)

Size Sleeve
21.5cm (8½in)   24.5cm (9¾in)   27.5cm (10¾in)

Yarn

Rowan Handknit Cotton x 50g balls

A. Tope	6	7	7
B. Red	1	1	1
C. Green	1	1	1

Needles

1 pair 3 ¼ mm (US 3) needles for edging
1 pair 4mm (US 6) needles for main body

Tension

20 sts and 28 rows to 10cm measured over patterned stocking stitch using 4 mm (US 6) needles

Back

Using 3 ¼ mm (US 3) needles and yarn A, cast on 66,74,82 sts and work from chart and written instructions as folls:
Chart row 1: K0,3,1, P1,2,2, (K4, P2) 10,11,13 times, K4,3,1, P1,0,0,
Chart row 2: P0,3,1, K1,2,2, (P4, K2) 10,11,12 times, P4,3 ,1 K1,0,0 .
Cont in rib from chart until row 14 completed
Change to 4mm (US 6) needles and beg with a

K row cont in patterned st st from chart, joining in and breaking off colours as indicated and using the intarsia technique for floral motifs as illustrated on page 27. Work from chart until row 58,60,64 completed.
Shape armhole
Cast off 6 sts at the beg next 2 rows. (54,62,70 sts)
Work until chart row 94,100,106 completed.
Shape shoulders and back neck
Cast off 4,5,6 sts at the beg next 2 rows.
Chart row 97,103,109: Cast off 4,5,6 sts, patt until 7,8,9 sts on RH needle, turn and leave rem sts on a holder.
Chart row 98,104,110: Cast off 3 sts, patt to end. Cast off rem 4,5,6 sts.
Slip centre 24,26,28 sts onto a holder, rejoin yarn to rem sts and patt to end. (11,13,15 sts)
Chart row 98,104,110: Cast off 4,5,6 sts, patt to end. (7,8,9 sts)
Chart row 99,105,111: Cast off 3 sts, patt to end. Cast off rem 4,5,6 sts.

Front

Work as for back until chart row 90,96,102 completed.
Shape front neck
Chart row 91,97,103: Patt 18,21,24 sts, turn and leave rem sts on a holder.
Chart row 92,98,104: Cast off 4 sts, patt to end. Dec 1 st at neck edge on next 2 rows. (12,15,18 sts)
Shape Shoulder
Chart row 95,101,107: Cast off 4,5,6 sts at beg next row and foll alt row.
Patt 1 row.
Cast off rem 4,5,6 sts.
Slip centre 18,20,22 sts onto a holder, rejoin yarn to rem sts and patt to end. (18,21,24 sts)
Patt 1 row
Chart row 93,99,105: Cast off 4 sts, patt to end. Dec 1 st at neck edge on next 2 rows. (12,15,18 sts)
Shape shoulder
Chart row 96,102,108: Cast off 4,5,6 sts at beg next row and foll alt row.
Patt 1 row.
Cast off rem 4,5,6 sts.

Sleeves (both alike)

Using 3 ¼ mm (US 3) needles and yarn A, cast on 34,36,38 sts and work from chart and written instructions as folls:
Chart row 1: K1,2,3, P2, (K4, P2) 5 times, K1,2,3.
Chart row 2: P1,2,3, K2,(P4, K2) 5 times, P1,2,3.
Cont in rib from chart until row 14 completed
Change to 4mm (US 6) needles and joining in and

breaking off colours as indicated on chart work in patterned st st using the intarsia technique for floral motifs, **do not work any incomplete motifs on sleeve.**
Chart row 15: Inc into first st, knit to last st, inc into last st. (36,38,40 sts)
Chart row 16: Purl.
Cont in patt from chart shaping sides by inc as indicated to 52,56,60 sts.
Work without further shaping until chart row 62,70,80 completed.
Cast off.

Press

all pieces as shown in making up instructions, page 48.

Neckband

Join right shoulder seam using backstitch.
Using 3 ¼ mm (US 3) needles and yarn A pick up and knit 9,10,11 sts down left front neck, knit across 18,20,22 sts on holder, pick up and knit 9,10,11 sts to shoulder and 3 sts down right back neck, knit across 24,26,28 sts on holder, pick up and knit 3 sts to shoulder. (66,72,78 sts)
Rib row 1 (WS row): K2, P4 to end.
Rib row 2 (RS row): K4, P2 to end.
Rep these 2 rows 4 times more.
Cast off in rib.
Complete sweater as shown in making up instructions page 48, leaving 14 rows at bottom edge of garment open for side vent.

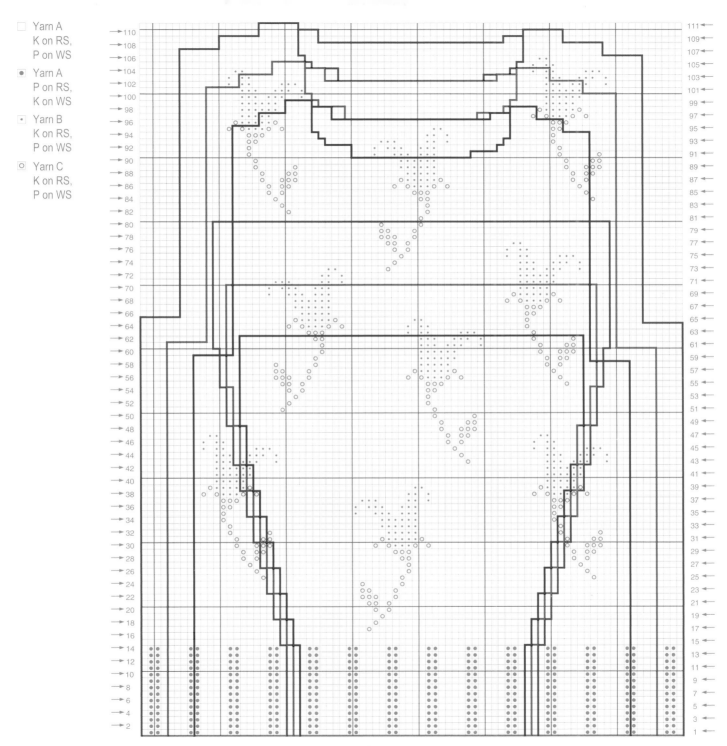

Yarn A
K on RS,
P on WS

Yarn A
P on RS,
K on WS

Yarn B
K on RS,
P on WS

Yarn C
K on RS,
P on WS

45

Cowboy waistcoat

Age 1-2 years 2-3 years 3-4 years

Size

Back

Front

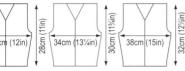

30.5cm (12in) 28cm (11in)
34cm (13¼in) 30cm (11¾in)
38cm (15in) 32cm (12½in)

Yarn
Rowan Wool Cotton x 50g balls

A. Dark Olive	3	3	3
B. Camel	1	1	1

Needles
1 pair 3 ¼ mm (US 3) needles for edging
1 pair 4mm (US 6) needles for main body

Buttons 5

Tension
22 sts and 30 rows to 10cm measured over pattern st st using 4mm (US 6) needles

Back
Using 3 ¼ mm (US 3) needles and yarn A, cast on 57,65,73 sts and work from chart and written instructions as folls:
Chart row 1: Knit.
Chart row 2: Knit.
Cont in garter st until chart row 6 completed.
Change to 4mm (US 6) needles, beg with a K row cont in st st, join in a separate length of yarn for each stripe using the intarsia technique as illustrated on page 27 and shape sides as folls:
Chart row 7: Inc into first st, patt to last st, inc into last st. (59,67,75 sts)

Cont from chart shaping sides by inc as indicated to 67,75,83 sts.
Work without further shaping until chart row 50,52,56 completed.
Shape armhole
Cast off 4 sts at the beg next 2 rows. (59,67,75 sts)
Dec 1 st at each end of next 3 rows and 2 foll alt rows. (49,57,65 sts)
Work 3 rows.
Dec 1 st at armhole edge on next row. (47,55,63 sts)
Cont in patt until chart row 86,92,98 completed.
Shape shoulders and back neck
Cast off 3,4,5 sts at the beg next 2 rows.
Chart row 89,95,101: Cast off 3,4,5 sts, patt until 6,7,8 sts on RH needle, turn and leave rem sts on a holder.
Chart row 90,96,102: Cast off 3 sts, patt to end. Cast off rem 3,4,5 sts.
Rejoin yarn and cast off centre 23,25,27 sts, patt to end. (9,11,13 sts)
Chart row 90,96,102: Cast off 3,4,5 sts, patt to end. (6,7,8 sts)
Chart row 91,97,103: Cast off 3 sts, patt to end. Cast off rem 3,4,5 sts.

Left Front
Using 3 ¼ mm (US 3) needles and yarn A, cast on 29,33,37 sts and work from chart and follow written instructions as follows:
Chart row 1: Knit.
Chart row 2: Knit.
Cont in garter st until chart row 6 completed.
Change to 4mm (US 6) needles, beg with a K row cont in st st, join in a separate length of yarn for each stripe using the intarsia technique, and shape side as folls:
Chart row 7: Inc into first st, patt to end. (30,34,38 sts)
Cont from chart, shaping side edge by inc as indicated to 34,38,42 sts.
Work without further shaping until chart row 50,52,56 completed.
Shape armhole
Cast off 4 sts at the beg next row. (30,34,38 sts)
Work 1 row.
Dec 1 st at armhole edge on next 3 rows and 2 foll alt rows. (25,29,33 sts)
Work 3 rows.
Complete armhole shaping and shape front neck
Chart row 63,65,69: Dec 1 st at each end of next row. (23,27,31 sts)
Cont to dec at neck edge on next 6 rows and then every foll alt row as indicated to 9,12,15 sts.
Work without further shaping until chart row 86,92,98 completed.

Shape shoulder
Cast off 3,4,5 sts at the beg next row and foll alt row.
Work 1 row
Cast off rem 3,4,5 sts.

Right Front
Using 3 ¼ mm (US 3) needles and yarn A, cast on 29,33,37 sts and work from chart and follow written instructions as follows:
Chart row 1: Knit.
Chart row 2: Knit.
Cont in garter st until chart row 6 completed
Change to 4mm (US 6) needles and complete to match left front, foll chart for right front and reversing shaping.

Press all pieces as shown in making up instructions, page 48.

Frontband
Join both shoulder seams using backstitch.
With RS of right front facing and using 3 ¼ mm (US 3) needles and yarn A, pick up and knit 43,45,49 sts from cast on edge to start of neck shaping, 22,24,26 sts up right front neck slope to shoulder, 29,31,33 sts across back neck, pick up and knit 22,24,26 sts down left front neck slope, and 43,45,49 sts to end. (159,169,183 sts)
Next row: Knit.
Buttonhole row (RS): Knit 119,125,135 sts, yo, K2tog (K7,8,9, yo, K2tog) 4 times, K2.
Knit 2 rows.
Cast off knitwise.

Armhole edgings (both alike)
With RS facing and using 3 ¼ mm needles and RS of garment facing pick up and knit 32,34,36 sts from side seam to shoulder and 32,34,36 sts down to side seam (64,68,72 sts)
Edging row 1 (WS row): Knit.
Edging row 2 (RS row): Knit.
Cast off knitwise.
Complete Waistcoat as shown in making up instructions, page 48.
Sew on buttons to correspond with buttonholes.

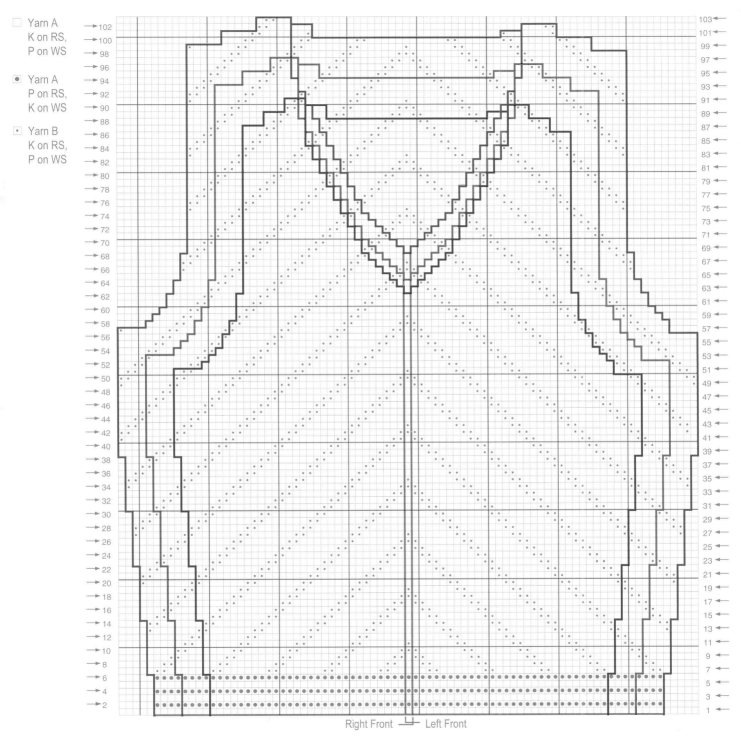

Knitting Techniques
A simple guide to making up and finishing

Putting your garment together

After spending many hours knitting it is essential that you complete your garment correctly. Following the written instructions and illustrations we show you how easy it is to achieve a beautifully finished garment; which will withstand the most boisterous child.

Pressing

With the wrong side of the fabric facing, pin out each knitted garment piece onto an ironing board using the measurements given in the size diagram. As each yarn is different, refer to the ball band and press pieces according to instructions given. Pressing the knitted fabric will help the pieces maintain their shape and give a smooth finish.

Sewing in ends

Once you have pressed your finished pieces, sew in all loose ends. Thread a darning needle with yarn, weave needle along approx 5 sts on wrong side of fabric; pull thread through. Weave needle in opposite direction approx 5 sts; pull thread through, cut end of yarn.

Making Up

If you are making a sweater join the right shoulder seam as instructed in the pattern, now work the neck edging. Join left shoulder seam and neck edging. If you are making a cardigan, join both shoulder seams as in the pattern and work edgings as instructed. Sew on buttons to correspond with buttonholes. Insert square set in sleeves as follows: Sew cast off edge of sleeve top into armhole. Making a neat right angle, sew in the straight sides at top of sleeve to cast off stitches at armhole. Join side and sleeve seams using either mattress stitch or back stitch. It is important to press each of the seams as you make the garment up.

Casting Off shoulder Seams together

This method secures the front and back shoulder stitches together, it also creates a small ridged seam. It is important that the cast off edge should by elastic like the rest of the fabric; if you find that your cast off is too tight, try using a larger needle. You can cast off with the seam on the right side (as illustrated) or wrong side of garment.

1. Place wrong sides of fabric together. Hold both needles with the stitches on in LH, insert RH needle into first stitch on both LH needles.

2. Draw the RH needle through both stitches.

3. Making one stitch on RH needle.

4. Knit the next stitch from both LH needles, two stitches on RH needle.

5. Using the point of one needle in LH, insert into first stitch on RH needle. Take the first stitch over the second stitch.

6. Repeat from 4. until one stitch left on right hand needle. Cut yarn and draw cut end through stitch to secure.

Picking Up Stitches

Once you have finished all the garment pieces, pressed them and sewn in all ends, you need to complete the garment by adding a neckband, front bands, or armhole edgings. This is done by picking up stitches along the edge of the knitted piece. The number of stitches to pick up is given in the pattern; these are made using a new yarn. When you pick up horizontally along a row of knitting it is important that you pick up through a whole stitch. When picking up stitches along a row edge, pick up one stitch in from the edge, this gives a neat professional finish.

1. Holding work in LH, with RS of fabric facing, insert RH needle into a whole stitch below the cast off edge, wrap new yarn around needle.

2. Draw the RH needle through fabric; making a loop with new yarn on right hand needle.

3. Repeat this action into the next stitch following the pattern instructions until all stitches have been picked up.

4. Work edging as instructed.

Mattress Stitch

This method of sewing up is worked on the right side of the fabric and is ideal for matching stripes. Mattress stitch should be worked one stitch in from edge to give the best finish. With RS of work facing, lay the two pieces to be joined edge to edge. Insert needle from WS between edge st and second st. Take yarn to opposite piece, insert needle from front, pass the needle under two rows, bring it back through to the front.

   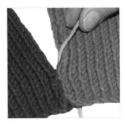

1. Work mattress stitch foundation as above.

2. Return yarn to opposite side working under two rows at a time, repeat.

3. At regular intervals gently pull stitches together.

4. The finished seam is very neat and almost impossible to see.

Back stitch

This method of sewing up is ideal for shoulder and armhole seams as it does not allow the fabric to stretch out of shape. Pin the pieces with right sides together. Insert needle into fabric at end, one stitch or row from edge, take the needle round the two edges securing them. Insert needle into fabric just behind where last stitch came out and make a short stitch. Re-insert needle where previous stitch started, bring up needle to make a longer stitch. Re-insert needle where last stitch ended, repeat to end taking care to match any pattern.

Sewing in a Zip

With right side facing, neatly match row ends and slip stitch fronts of garment together. Pin zip into place, with right side of zip to wrong side of garment, matching centre front of garment to centre of zip. Neatly backstitch into place using a matching coloured thread. Undo slip stitches, zip inserted.

Rowan Overseas Distributors

AUSTRALIA : Australian Country Spinners, 314 Albert Street, Brunswick, Victoria 3056. Tel : (03) 9380 3888

BELGIUM : Pavan, Koningin Astridlaan 78, B9000 Gent. Tel : (32) 9 221 8594
E mail: pavan@pandora.be

CANADA: Diamond Yarn, 9697 St Laurent, Montreal, Quebec, H3L 2N1. Tel :(514) 388 6188
Diamond Yarn (Toronto), 155 Martin Ross, Unit 3, Toronto, Ontario,M3J 2L9. Tel :(416) 736 6111
E mail: diamond@diamondyarn.com

DENMARK : Please contact Rowan for stockist details.

FRANCE : Elle Tricot, 8 Rue du Coq, 67000 Strasbourg. Tel : (33) 3 88 23 03 13.
E mail: elletricot@wanadoo.fr

GERMANY : Wolle & Design, Wolfshovener Strasse 76, 52428 Julich-Stetternich. Tel : (49) 2461 54735.
E mail : Wolle_und_Design@t-online.de

HOLLAND : de Afstap, Oude Leliestraat 12, 1015 AW Amsterdam. Tel : (31) 20 6231445.

HONG KONG : East Unity Co Ltd, Unit B2, 7/F, Block B, Kailey Industrial Centre, 12 Fung Yip Street, Chai Wan. Tel : (852) 2869 7110.

ICELAND : Storkurinn, Kjorgardi, Laugavegi 59, Reykjavik. Tel : (354) 551 82 58.

JAPAN : Puppy Co Ltd, TOC Building, 7-22-17 Nishigotanda, Shinagawa-ku, Tokyo. Tel : (81) 3 3494 2395.
E mail: webmaster@puppyarn.co.jp

KOREA : My Knit Studio, (3F) 121 Kwan Hoon Dong, Chongro-ku, Seoul. Tel : (82) 2 722 0006

NEW ZEALAND : Please contact Rowan for stockist details.

NORWAY : Pa Pinne, Tennisvn 3D, 0777 Oslo. Tel : (47) 909 62 818.
E mail : design@paapinne.no

SWEDEN : Wincent, Norrtulsgaten 65, 11345 Stockholm. Tel : (46) 8 673 70 60 Fax: (46) 8 33 70 68.
E mail: wincent@chello.se

TAIWAN : Il Lisa International Trading Co Ltd, No 181, Sec 4, Chung Ching N. Road, Taipei, Taiwan R.O.C. Tel : (886) 2 8221 2925.
Chien He Wool Knitting Co, 10 -1 313 Lane, Sec 3, Cmung-Ching North Road, Taipei, Taiwan. Tel : (886) 2 2596 0269

U.S.A.: Rowan USA, 4 Townsend West, Suite 8, Nashua, New Hampshire 03063. Tel : (1 603) 886 5041 / 5043.
E mail : wfibers@aol.com

UNITED KINGDOM : Green Lane Mill, Holmfirth,West Yorkshire, HD9 2DX. Tel : (44) (0) 1484 681881.
Email : mail@knitrowan.com